Behind The Cross

Is This Christ's Ministry

Or Yours?

Behind The Cross:
Is This Christ's Ministry Or Yours?
By
Harvey Jones

Published by Greater Works Enterprises
www.greaterworksenterprises.com
2019

First Printing: 2019

ISBN 978-0-9975643-6-5

Greater Works Enterprises
Website: www.greaterworksenterprises.com

Scripture quotations taken from The Holy Bible, King James Version, Cambridge, 1769.

Acknowledgments

I praise and thank God for his mercy, grace, love and bountiful blessings. God inspired and permitted me to write this book and I believe it is His will that it be shared with His people, especially those in leadership in His Kingdom.

To my parents Johnnie and Ella Jones who taught me to believe in and have faith in God.

To my loving wife who has stood by my side for over 46 years loving me, praying for me and supporting me in my endeavors.

My tenure in the military, has afforded me the opportunity to have several Pastors; to my Pastors, past and present, whose inspirational teaching and guidance has developed me into a vessel that God is using for His Glory.

To Satan, I remind you that you are a defeated foe and you have no authority or power of me; that even though you are constantly a stumbling block, greater is He that is within me than he that is in the world. I have been given power over you and you are under my feet. I am victorious because of the blood of Jesus the Christ, the Son of the Living God.

To all those who read this book, thank you and may the God of all comfort always be with you, lead you and guide you. May you strive to reach the mark of a higher calling in Christ Jesus our Lord.

TABLE OF CONTENTS

Preface

Church Leaders, particularly Pastors have allowed the walls of spiritual and moral integrity to crumble to the point that our church's standards are a mirror image of the world's standards. The result in many churches is the church has become entertaining, exploitive and irrelevant. The way we dress, our speech, conduct, and the music we play and listen to is no different than what is in existence outside the church. Sadly, the way we treat each other in the church is often worse than the way sinners treat each other in the world. There are many things going on in our churches 'Behind the Cross' which are not aligned with God's Word. Church leaders today have allowed the world's secular morals, values, and political influence to infiltrate and weaken the church's ability to shine the light of Jesus in darkness and continually salt a world that has lost its savor. The citizens of our communities are suffering, and our community's churches lack the sensitivity, concern, and willingness to proactively address the issues and problems that are destroying our society. Church leaders are more concerned with impressing celebrities, politicians and gaining notoriety with the public and the news media than fulfilling the Great Commission.

Pastors frequently make the statement that they don't believe in or condone 'respecting persons' but their actions are not commensurate with that principle. Church leaders are encouraged to read this book and take an objective look at not only what they are doing but the reasons why and the methods they are deploying to shepherd God's people. It is my heartfelt hope that if you see yourself or your ministry not fulfilling the Great Commission and you can identify your actions with any of the deficiencies described in this book, you will not be offended but provoked to reconsider your current methodology and make the necessary adjustments to ensure what you are doing and how you are doing it is pleasing God.

Chapter 1
What's Going on in Our Churches?

It is written:

Matthew 5:13

Ye are the salt of the earth: but if the salt has lost his savor,

wherewith shall it be salted? it is thenceforth good for nothing,

but to be cast out, and to be trodden under foot of men.

Most if not all Christian Churches display the
cross in some form either physically or in the
ministry's stated ordinances of what they believe.
The cross is a symbol and beacon of hope that shines
bright and draws saints and sinners to a place of
repentance. The church experience for the believer
should be refreshing, rewarding, energizing and
motivating the believer to love God and their

neighbors as themselves, and to go into the world to win souls for Christ. Though displayed at the forefront the cross is often used as a facade that camouflages hidden agendas. The cross of Jesus is an emblem of suffering and shame and the place where Jesus paid the ultimate price for our redemption from sin, death, hell and the grave. Christ is not displeased so much with what we are doing in our churches but with the why and the how we conduct ourselves (our ways). In the pages of this book, I share some of my experiences of what goes on behind the cross. The problems of lying, deceit, jealousy, envy, backbiting, strife and all manner of sin and evil in our churches do not originate in the church but they have found their way in and now permeates our churches like a plague of cancerous rats and roaches. Currently, there is a lack of integrity, both spiritually and morally in existence from the White House to the poor house, from the church house to my house and yes in even in your house. We who call ourselves Christians have failed to surrender our wills for the will of God and refuse to be led by the Holy Spirit. In our daily walk, we assimilate into the world around us and fail to take a stand for Christ. In our society, it is acceptable to use profane and vulgar language, dress provocatively, pierce and tattoo any part of our anatomy and commit any sinful act that satisfies our sinful flesh. We bring our socially acceptable conduct into the church and contaminate it with our sIn.

You notice that I capitalize the I in the word sIn, I do this to emphasize that I am the problem, not others. The I is for self and if we replace the I with an O the word becomes "son." If we are truly committed to Christ and the Word of God, we would change our conduct and walk according to His will and not ours. If we were more concerned with others and less concerned with our own agendas; we would be conducting ourselves like the Son of God. If all peoples of this world would act like the Son of God there would be no need for the military, police or the justice system because we'd treat everyone with respect and love. The primary problem is Christians don't let their walk match their talk. Have you ever wondered why it seems as though our male choir directors and many of our male musicians are not married and seem to be confused about their sexuality? Is it the spirit of Lucifer or what? They appear to get along very well with women but appear to avoid getting close to men in a platonic relationship. They appear to have female tendencies, mannerisms, and characteristics. That seems 'queer' to me, I'm just saying. Churches are full of sincere people who love the Lord and strive to live for Him. Unfortunately, the masses don't follow the precepts and commands of God as evidenced by their conduct, demeanor and lack of integrity which has permeated and infected the church. This sin infestation is fully operational from the pulpit to the parking lot. The church's mission and the mission of every Christian is plainly stated in Matthew 28:19-20; *Go ye therefore, and teach all nations, baptizing them in the name of the Father, and of the Son, and of the Holy Ghost: teaching them to observe all things whatsoever I have commanded you: and, lo, I am with you always, even unto the end of the world. Amen.*

If there is no overwhelming evidence of the mission being accomplished in every facet of the ministry, the church is failing. There is a great need for brotherly love and compassion in all our communities. Our community's churches have all the resources necessary to satisfy many if not all the community's needs. If churches worked together there would be no need for governmental social service programs for housing, food, mental health, and medical care. Unfortunately, if you put a group of church Pastors in a room to develop and implement a program to meet the needs of the community; the meeting turns into a bickering 'Junkyard Dog' fiasco competition to determine which dog has the loudest bark, who gets to be the 'Big Dog' with the bone. They interject their personal agendas, selfish pride, jealousy and envy which ends in a contest of who's in charge, who gets the credit, the news media coverage and takes the bone home; the result, the community suffers by not having its needs met. "When the power of love overcomes the love of power, the world will know peace" - Jimi Hendrix. However, William Gladstone once said (prior to Hendrix): "We look forward to the time when the Power of Love will replace the Love of Power. Then will our world know the blessings of peace (William Gladstone 1809-1898)." There is just as much politics in the church as in corporate America. Church leadership claims to operate on spiritual principles but the reality is they operate just like their worldly counterparts by utilizing the 'friends and family plan' when giving opportunities for ministry and making appointments.

Many of our so-called 'Word' churches have an established executive board that consists of spouses, brothers, sisters, in-laws, and children; this is nepotism in its purest form. Church leaders avoid conflicts and rarely exercise conflict resolution. It has been my experience that when problems arise within a ministry that involves a single individual, the ministry leadership refuses to confront the person and deal with the issue but rather chooses to ignore the problem in hopes it will resolve itself or just go away. I served in the U. S. Marines for over 20 years; Marines run to the sound of the gunfire and never retreat. Marines improvise, adapt and overcome, facing the problems they encounter and mitigate the situation by any means necessary. Church leaders are not Marines, but they claim to be part of God's Army. The operational functions of Christians and military warriors are more similar than different. Christians have been called, appointed, anointed by God and infused with the Holy Spirit to stand their ground and overcome evil and sin by the power of Christ. God requires Pastors to nurture and care for those He has assigned to them, but many Pastors are cowards and avoid many issues they encounter for fear of losing their popularity among the parishioners. This is especially true when Pastors are confronted with issues that involve their members that are major contributors. This is what I call the ultimate 'fear factor' for a Pastor; they don't want to offend their major contributors. Somehow, they have forgotten that God is their source, not man. The way most Pastors and church leaders react to problems I doubt if they really believe what they preach and teach concerning the source of blessings. I fail to understand why some churches have a Pastor and a co-pastor, usually but not always the co-pastor is the Pastor's spouse. I am not the most intelligent person on the planet, but I have concluded that anything with two heads is a freak. We can avoid many of our self-inflicted problems by adhering to God's Word. It is written,

1 Corinthians 11:3

But I would have you know, that the head of every man is Christ; and the head of the woman is the man; and the head of Christ is God.

This chain of command or authority is very plain to me, so why the confusion? By the way, I personally have no problem with women ministers or preachers but only have one thing to say about women pastors. It is written:

1 Timothy 3:1-7

This is a true saying, if a man desires the office of a bishop, he desired a good work. A bishop then must be blameless, the husband of one wife, vigilant, sober, of good behaviour, given to hospitality, apt to teach; not given to wine, no striker, not greedy of filthy lucre; but patient, not a brawler, not covetous; one that ruleth well his own house, having his children in subjection with all gravity; (For if a man know not how to rule his own house, how shall he take care of the church of God?) Not a novice, lest being lifted up with pride he falls into the condemnation of the devil. Moreover he must have a good report of them which are without; lest he fall into reproach and the snare of the devil.

Chapter 2
<u>Church Worship Service</u>

If you are like me, you have become fed up with the animated cartoon we call 'having church'. Many churchgoers jump, run, shout, and foam at the mouth but at the end of the service they cannot recall any part of the message and have no substance with which they can overcome the desires of their flesh and defeat the devil. Church should be a filling station where Christians can get recharged with the Word of God and inspired by the Holy Spirit to go and serve God by meeting the needs of others. Give God the sacrifice of praise when the Spirit moves you; shout, jump, run, praise and clap, but only when the Spirit moves you not just because it is the thing to do. Churchgoers have one existence or facade for the church and another for the world. In Hinduism, an avatar is a deliberate descent of a deity to earth or a descent of the supreme being. In the animated science fiction movie entitled 'Avatar' humans transfer their conscientiousness into an alien body in order to interact with the inhabitants of the planet. Churchgoers are very similar in that they transform themselves into what they perceive to be a Christian and enter the church with a different conduct, speech, and overall demeanor than what they display when not in church. When in church they act like animated cartoon characters playing 'Simon says'. Simon says-- lift your hands, Simon says stand up, jump, shout, run around the church, tell your neighbor this and tell your neighbor that; give the Lord a hand of praise for this and give the Lord a hand of praise for that. Why can't the minister just preach and teach the inspired Word of God and the worshippers respond when lead by the Holy Spirit? In a lot of churches what is referred to as praise and worship sounds more like a rock concert, too loud and distorted to the point that you cannot understand or receive the spiritual blessing from it. The sound system in a church should amplify the voice to a level that will ensure the speaker, singer or musicians are heard but not at a level of deafening distorted sound.

Then there's the 'Super Saints', those who say 'Praise the Lord' in every sentence, they run, jump and shout at every service but when the Devil shows up they are first in line to join him in creating discord, disharmony, confusion and basically messing up the church. These 'Super Saints' are so spiritual they have become no earthly good. There seem to be no standards or spiritual qualifiers for ministering to the congregation; if you have talent you are permitted to perform regardless of your lifestyle, spiritual and moral integrity. In many churches whether you conduct yourself like a heathen has no bearing and does not affect your qualifications for ministry. The standards have been all but eliminated in the modern church. You can be vulgar, obscene, disrespectful, and disobedient to God's Word and living in sIn and still permitted to minister in the church. Even preachers feel it necessary to express themselves with the use of profanity or vulgar terms in order to make a point or to be humorous. I have always considered the use of inappropriate language a display of one's inability to effectively utilize the English language; it's all about choices, you can choose to use obscene or vulgar language or not, it's just that simple. While serving as a United States Marine Corps Drill Instructor at the Marine Corps Recruit Depot located at Parris Island, South Carolina, which is considered one of the toughest and most demanding training facilities in the world, I was known as the only DI that did not use profanity in my training of Marine recruits. It was a decision I made for respect for myself, for God and all those within the sound of my voice. Officers and Staff Noncommissioned officers from other parts of Depot would come and observe me training the recruits to see if what they heard about me was true. I can assure you they were amazed at my ability to be as tough and demanding as other DIs and not curse while performing my duties as a Marine DI and as a physical training, close combat instructor. Therefore, I conclude that ministers of the Gospel of Jesus are without an excuse when they choose to use profane, obscene and vulgar language. It is written,

James 3:10

Out of the same mouth proceedeth blessing and cursing. My

brethren, these things ought not so to be.

What in the world have we come to?

Chapter 3
Money Matters

Many ministers have perfected their ability to 'shear the sheep' and collect large offerings at will. I believe in prophecy, but many Pastors and prophets preface the offering with a so-called prophetic word about seeing someone with a new house, car or a large financial blessing. When this is stated you can hear parishioners claiming the new car or house and when the time to give is proclaimed, they begin digging in their wallets and purses to get their offering together. The bait is a prophetic word that promises a new material thing, the hook is set and then swallowed by the unwitting sheep. The allocations of funds for programs within the ministry are not always distributed where there's need but to the entity, person or persons that has the most clout or favor within the ministry. The purpose of the church is to gather the saints of God in worship and praise and to educate, train and equip the saints for the work of the ministry. Churches should be provoking parishioners to good works. In many churches, the focus is on what will attract favorable media attention and gain notoriety for the Pastor. Many churches spend thousands of dollars paying for guest artists, ministers, teachers, prophets, life coaches and motivational speaker's transportation, food, lodging and honorariums or fees, but neglect and fail to develop and utilize the gifts already within their ministries. A vast majority of funds are allocated for speakers to conduct training or workshops but what is shared by the visiting speaker is often ignored by Pastors and church leaders who continue business as usual. It is a waste of funds and foolishness to continue year after year to pay someone to come and share with your ministry, give you a 'God Breathed' Word and instructions from God then ignore the instructions given. The selection of ministry and church staff workers is often based on the 'friends and family plan' and dictates the amount of compensation they are paid. Rarely are there any genuine position descriptions and job requirements utilized in hiring practices but rather how they are favored by the Pastor.

Many of those working full-time as church staff have little or no experience or competence in performing their assigned tasks but are loyal 'yes men and women' and willing to work for low pay and little or no compensation plan that includes any sort of benefits; resulting in the church getting the quality of worker it is paying for. There are many competent, qualified and spirit-filled believers willing to work for the church but they are not wanted because they may not be willing to just go along to get along or be compensated below a level of what they should be paid for their service. In most churches the 'laborer is worthy of his hire' only applies to the Pastor. A church or ministry that compensates the Pastor to an economic level that allows him to live the good life but fails to ensure the same for all full-time staff members is a disgrace. Pastors and often church staff take advantage of parishioners by making unethical loans and receiving gifts. The laborer is worthy of his hire, but many popular, well-known preachers now demand a certain amount of money before they will speak at your meeting. It appears that some have placed a price tag on the Gospel and just like at a fast-food eatery they demand payment before you are served.

Chapter 4
<u>What Are You Wearing?</u>

Many pastors feel it necessary to be 'G-Q' (suave or well-dressed) and dressed according to the current trends in fashion as dictated by society. Some, however, have taken this to an extreme resulting in attire that is a flamboyant, showy, gaudy and an empty ostentatious display. The attire of many ministers when performing his or her duties, especially from the pulpit should not be a distraction causing parishioners to pay more attention to what he or she is wearing than the message or what is being taught. Gaudy jewelry and other devices are inappropriate when ministering. The attire of a minister does not have to be cheap or inexpensive but should be sober and tasteful. The wearing of robes by the clergy eliminates a lot of problems and confusion concerning what to wear. But even in that, preachers have developed the art of decorating robes to the point of lunacy. Some churchgoers especially women, dress as if they are going to a night club and trolling for men. I suppose that's okay at first because you are to come as you are; but at some point, the Holy Spirit should convict you and help you to realize that certain attire is inappropriate not only in church but in any setting. Proper fitting and tasteful appropriate proper attire for the church and anywhere should be your norm. Standards for appropriate attire are important for men, women, boys, and girls. The young men in the current American culture believe it to be appropriate to wear their trousers and pants below their waistline, even to the point of showing their underwear. It is my understanding that this practice began in the prisons and was a sign that you are ready and willing to participate in unnatural sexual relations with another man; now how gross is that? Women in the church should not require a lap cloth but their clothing should be an appropriate length and a non-revealing fit. The designers ensure most of the clothing available is too short, too low and too tight.

Proverbs 11:22

As a jewel of gold in a swine's snout, so is a fair woman which is without discretion.

Likewise, men should ensure a proper fit of their clothing that does not reveal any intimate part of their anatomy. Unfortunately, this ripped jean, tattooed, pierced, skimpy dressed generation feels they can wear anything they want anywhere they want, anytime they want. Basically, there is a lack of respect for self, others, and for the House of God. Men wear their hats inside the church and have no principles concerning their attire. Most but not all men will respect the sanctuary during actual worship services but feel it acceptable to wear their hats or caps in the church when there's no service being conducted. The sanctuary should be respected as a holy place where we meet the Lord, not just some building where we meet, and it is then during worship service is transformed into a holy place. We are the vessels of the Holy Spirit and must conduct ourselves in a manner that always displays our respect for God and His Holy Temple. Both men and women have lost respect for the Holy things of God.

The level of respect you show for yourself, your God and for others must not be limited to the sanctuary or just Sundays but should be reflective of your life anytime, anyplace and anywhere. I was always taught to respect God's Temple, the church, Pastors now seem to accept any standards the world wants to dictate, they won't challenge or stand up against these 'little foxes' in the church. It is written,

1 Peter 3:3-4

Whose adorning let it not be that outward adorning of plaiting the hair, and of wearing of gold, or of putting on of

apparel; but let it be the hidden man of the heart, in that which is not corruptible, even the ornament of a meek and quiet spirit, which is in the sight of God of great price.

And that's all I've got to say about that.

Chapter 5
<u>Discipline</u>

Where is the discipline in the church and does it still exist? In the military there often exists a promotion policy referred to as 'FUMU', Foul Up, Move Up. In Corporate America and now in the church people who display problems are often promoted when their current status is not in line with God's Word. The premise that's often stated is that none of us are perfect and if God only used perfect people none of us would be used by God because none of us are worthy. I agree that all of us have fallen short of where God desires for us to be but there should not be any reward for sIn. People who willfully continue in sIn should be confronted, counseled and directed to a path of righteousness and not promoted to a leadership position in the church or permitted to minister to His people while continually and willfully living in sIn. When God gives us the opportunity to let our light shine on the world's stage, we often waste it by conforming to the world's standards. Parishioners are not as naive and stupid as some Pastors think, we see what's going on but choose to remain quiet and pray that the Lord will eventually correct the absurd, ridiculous and foolish handling of His church and His people. Some church members get so fed up with what they observe that they feel obligated to look elsewhere for a place to worship. Pastors will soon stand before God and must answer for the hurt and pain they have caused due to their inability or unwillingness to address issues in the church.

1 Corinthians 6:2

Do ye not know that the saints shall judge the world? and if the world shall be judged by you, are ye unworthy to judge the smallest matters?

Church goers habitually accuse others of 'judging' but if I point out to you that your shoes are untied I have identified a deficiency that could cause you to trip and injure yourself or if I tell you to get out of the road because a truck is coming I have warned you of an oncoming threat. Neither of those examples is considered judging but I am simply pointing out a situation that if not corrected may cause you harm or possibly physical death. Likewise, identifying a problem for a fellow believer is not judging but helping you to see a problem that could cause you harm and if not physical and more importantly spiritual death.

In some churches, unwed mothers must stand before the congregation and apologize to the church for their sexual sins. The world and our society refer to the unborn child as illegitimate; the illegitimacy is the parents. In my opinion, there's no such thing as an illegitimate child only illegitimate parent. The practice of having the mother stand before the congregation to ask forgiveness for her sins is ludicrous and is only an exercise in futility that does not benefit anyone except the gossips in the church.

I would ask where the man is who participated is in this unlawful act of sexual sIn. We all make mistakes, but Pastors and other church leadership are even taking advantage of young women, getting them pregnant, leaving their wives for another woman, stealing the church's money and basically committing all manner of sIn and evil. Where has the fear and holy reverence gone? Pastor's wives often get either dissatisfied or disgusted and refuse to support her husband and watch his back when she should be his most diligent 'prayer warrior' and intercessor. On the other hand, some Pastor's wives get high-minded and think they have as much authority as the Pastor and attempt to exercise their unauthorized authority among the parishioners.

When the Pastor does not put a stop to this it leads to confusion and discord among the members of the church. Churches make rules, share them with the congregation and don't enforce them or hold parishioners accountable or challenge them when they don't follow the rules. Frequently the rules fail to be followed because those on the front line of the ministry are the primary violators of the rules that have been established. How can Pastors expect their members to adhere to policy when those on their staff or in leadership don't follow the rules? Often exceptions are made for those who are prominent within the community because of their social, economic, or political status. The rules are only applicable to those who are not high enough on the 'food chain' or church hierarchy. If you have certain positions of favor, you can do no wrong. Your suggestions are always accepted and acted upon regardless of the correct, moral and spiritual ramifications that ensue because of their recommendation. Many Pastors fail to realize that success in the world's arena does not equate to success in God's Kingdom. It does, however, mean that the successful person has been blessed by God and has the potential to become a success for God in the work of the ministry. Without a working knowledge of God's Word and a true revelation of God via a personal relationship with Jesus Christ, no individual's success in the world automatically qualify him or her for a leadership position in the Church of the Living God. The world's wisdom does not compare to God's wisdom.

1 Corinthians 3:18-19

Let no man deceive himself. If any man among you seemeth to be wise in this world, let him become a fool, that he may be wise. For the wisdom of this world is foolishness with God. For it is written, He taketh the wise in their own craftiness.

I have learned that a fool cannot be reasoned with. "But what a fool believes he sees no wise man has the power to reason away" - Michael McDonald.

Chapter 6
In House Ministry

The first ministry of any church must be to its members, but many churches fail in this because of the notoriety they seek is in the community, news media, and other church leaders. Many of the ministries within a church exist in name only and fail to meet the needs of those it is established to help. Many churches have Couples Ministry, Singles Ministry, Youth Ministry and Children's Ministry. Those ministries have an organized structure, conduct planning meetings but don't help the people. In other words, they have the form of Godliness but deny the power thereof. When you see men carrying themselves as women and women carrying themselves like men, there's a problem that needs to be addressed. When marriages are ending in divorce, there's a problem. When singles are living together before marriage, there's a problem. When men and women are having sex outside of marriage, there's a problem. When singles are producing children out of wedlock, there's a problem. When men attend church for years, sitting under the anointing and seemingly receiving the Word of God but are still switching and twitching like a woman; and likewise, when women are carrying themselves like a man and none show any signs of deliverance, there's a problem. When the children we've reared in a Christian home choose to go astray by living in sIn, there's a problem.

Children and young adults have no fear; no fear of their parents, no fear of the police, no fear of contracting sexually transmitted diseases, no fear of some stranger piercing holes in or putting ink on any part of their anatomy and no fear of God. Our daughters open their legs for any Tom, Dick or Harry they meet, and our sons will deposit their sperm into any willing female that they encounter. Our daughters choose to live in sIn and our sons take on a concubine. When men are having unnatural relationships with men and women having unnatural relationships with women; we need Jesus in our in-house ministries. It is written,

James 3:17

But the wisdom that comes from heaven is first of all pure; then peace-loving, considerate, submissive, full of mercy and good fruit, impartial and sincere.

We have established ministries within our churches but are they functional and are they bearing fruit? We need to stop lying to ourselves and to God and strive to meet the needs of His people; first to those within the church, then to those outside the church.

Chapter 7
Church Meetings

I have had the fortune or misfortune, depending upon your point of view, to be part of ministries and churches in Alabama, North Carolina, Georgia, Florida, Washington, DC, Hawaii and Beirut, Lebanon. I personally dislike meetings, especially when we are meeting just to say we had a meeting. Any meeting should have an agenda and provide information necessary for the attendees to become more productive in all endeavors relating to the stated purpose of the meeting. When a meeting is held to read information, I consider that meeting unnecessary because I can read information myself. That sort of meeting could have been omitted by simply sending the information to me via email or placing the document in my hand. In some of the church business meetings I've attended, I have heard Deacons and other leaders make threats, such as, just wait until I go to my truck and get my pistol or we are not here to abide by what the Bible says, we're here to abide by Robert's Rules of Order. At one church I attended the Deacons called a meeting inviting people that never attend church but are registered as church members; the meeting they held resulted in the pulpit being declared vacant and the Pastor fired. The following day the headlines in the local newspaper read: "Church Tells Pastor to Go Tell It on Someone Else's Mountain." In other meetings, there has been a purpose stated but the meeting ends up being something totally different. If you call a prayer meeting, you should pray. Often prayer meetings turn into pep rallies or a gathering of parishioners to perform some other task the church desires to accomplish usually related to manual labor. Choir rehearsals turn in to forum for complaints. Bible study has become a platform for the designated teacher to express their spiritual prowess and offers little or no opportunity for feedback or interaction with attendees. When you attend a Bible study you should be able to discuss the Bible not just receive a lecture. Even in national meetings or conferences, I have observed delegates who attend conventions at the expense of their church but utilize their time to partying and going on cruises when they should be at meetings representing their ministry. In committee meetings I have attended at various churches, attendees belittle and disrespect other church members. This sort of verbal abuse is tolerated by leadership and causes one to ask is this how the Lord wants us to conduct ourselves? I would respond with a loud NO! Pastors talk a good game when under the anointing and speaking from the pulpit illuminating the cross of Christ but what really goes on behind the cross is a dishonor to the Kingdom of God. Meetings should be held to develop ideas, discuss events and strategies that will facilitate reaching the world for the Lord, not to disrespect and debase others. Unfortunately, some Pastors use their pulpits as a platform to disrespect others during their sermons. "Great minds discuss ideas; Average minds discuss events; Small minds discuss people" -

Eleanor Roosevelt

Chapter 8
<u>Fixing What's Behind The Cross</u>

How Can We Fix What Goes on in the Church 'Behind the Cross'? The underlining problem is sIn, each of us must look inside ourselves, weigh our thoughts and actions, acknowledge that the problems exist, seek the Father's guidance and strive to accomplish His will in every aspect of our lives. The biggest obstacle to overcoming our problems within the church is the Pastor's fear and lack of trust of others which results in his unwillingness to hear from and receive anything from those God has given him to lead. I emphatically agree that the Pastor should receive his instructions from God and pass on those instructions to his congregation. I also conclude that the lines of communication must be open, and the Pastor must be receptive to input from his membership. The Pastor is God's man, but he is not God. Many churchgoers sacrifice their time, energy and financial resources in the church of their choice, but the ultimate sacrifice is when we obey the voice of God given through His prophets and His Holy Word. It is written,

1 Samuel 15:22

And Samuel said, Hath the LORD as great delight in burnt offerings and sacrifices, as in obeying the voice of the LORD? Behold, to obey is better than sacrifice, and to hearken than the fat of rams.

What many churchgoers fail to realize is that Pastors and other ministers regardless of their self-proclaimed or appointed title of Bishop, Prophet, Apostle, Reverend, Doctor, Priest, Rabbi or Pope; they are all just men with the God-given ability to choose. Each person has a choice to sIn or live holy. Men can and will often fail to live up to your expectations. Therefore, parishioners must not put the totality of their trust in any man. Everything you hear and see in life must be weighed against the Word of God and then acted upon as led by the Holy Spirit. Christians need to stop the 'monkey see, monkey do' activity they participate in when they are in church. New members and converts observe what others do that appears to be what the Pastor wants, and they begin doing the same. In other words, they display the character traits they observe in church just to fit in and seem normal in the church environment. The character they display in church is far from their true character and is just a mask they wear in church. The true person exists at home, work and play. In order to change your character, you must change your thoughts from the world's way to God's way. The beginning of this transformation must have its basis in the Word of God. Christians must feed their spirit man daily with the Word of God; that means read your Bible, pray and seek God's presence daily. Once you've fed your spirit- man with God's Word you must strive each moment of the day to live in compliance with Gods' commandments. Pastors need to stop allowing the politics, backbiting, and childish bickering that exists in today's churches.

They need to hold members accountable and confront sIn and disobedience when and where and in whomever it exists.

If Pastors continue to ignore the obvious sInful lifestyles of their membership, the lack of love and respect displayed among members and the disrespect shown toward God, His people, and His church will continue to be bound by sIn and not effective in accomplishing the mission of Christ. Pastors must not fear delegating authority to others while retaining the responsibility for the outcome. Pastors must hold their leaders accountable and ensure effective programs are developed within the ministry to ensure all facets of the church have a resource developed for the needs of their demographic. Just having a ministry listed with team members is not enough; the ministry must be active, effective and be held accountable by the Pastor to meet the needs of the members and the community. Too many churches have ministries, but the ministry fails to accomplish any good or meet the needs of God's people. The fault with these problems lies with each of us, but within the church environment, the fault and blame rests with God's man, the Pastor. He must be led by God and not afraid to confront and deal with issues of sin and inappropriate conduct whenever and wherever it occurs in the ministry. If the Pastor is leading us in the direction God wants, then we are obligated to follow. How do you know if the Pastor is leading you the way God wants? Pray and weigh his leadership and direction with God's Word. When we believe that the Pastor or the leadership within the church is wrong it is our responsibility to pray for God's intervention and hope and believe God will reveal His plan to the Pastor who will in turn act accordingly. Many parishioners believe it's their responsibility to correct the Pastor by correcting him themselves. Parishioners write letters or send emails voicing their disagreement with a specific issue or occurrence. The action parishioners should take is to pray and believe that God will make the necessary corrections within the church and make all things work together for the good of all concerned. Anyone not willing to respond in prayer and faith to problems they encounter within the church needs to find another place to worship where they feel their needs both spiritually and emotionally are being met. It is written:

1 Chronicles 16:22

Saying, Touch not mine anointed, and do my prophets no harm.

The people of God have a tremendous responsibility to fulfill Christ's mission by walking in love with all mankind, unfortunately, we are currently failing. Let's get it together people; we can start by, sowing and reaping.

Sow a thought, reap an action.

Sow an action, reap a habit.

Sow a habit reap a character.

Sow a character, reap a destiny.

What should the church be doing?

John 6:38-40

For I came down from heaven, not to do mine own will, but the will of him that sent me. And this is the Father's will which hath sent me, that of all which he hath given me I should lose nothing, but should raise it up again at the last day. And this is the will of him that sent me, that every one which seeth the Son, and believeth on him, may have everlasting life: and I will raise him up at the last day.

If you sincerely want to straighten out the chaos in the church, you only need to find a mirror, look into it and you'll see the problem; fix that person and the problems will cease to exist. What have we come to? The answers are found in the Word of God, for it is written: This know also, that in the last days perilous times shall come.

2 Timothy 3:1-5

For men shall be lovers of their own selves, covetous, boasters, proud, blasphemers, disobedient to parents, unthankful, unholy, without natural affection, trucebreakers, false accusers, incontinent, fierce, despisers of those that are good, Traitors, heady, high-minded, lovers of pleasures more than lovers of God; Having a form of godliness, but denying the power thereof: from such turn away.

My heart's desire is for all men to receive the salvation and redemption offered to them by accepting Jesus the Christ in their heart as Lord and Savior.

Chapter 9
Our Fellowships

KOINONIA: The Greek definition of the word Koinonia literally means Christian fellowship or body of believers or an intimate spiritual communion and participative sharing in a common religious commitment and spiritual community.

Acts 2:44-47

And all that believed were together and had all things common; And sold their possessions and goods, and parted them to all men, as every man had need. And they, continuing daily with one accord in the temple, and breaking bread from house to house, did eat their meat with gladness and singleness of heart, Praising God, and having favour with all the people. And the LORD added to the church daily such as should be saved.

Can we as believers say that we are truly living epistles of God's Word and truly living according to His will? We may have small clicks, but we are not altogether with respect to Koinonia. The children in the neighborhood where I grew up adhered to certain rules and standards; one was the 'Rule of the Street lights.' The streetlights in my town would come on as dusk or the period of partial darkness between day and night. The lights on the poles in my neighborhood would make a popping sound and begin to glow, when they were fully operational they would make a final buzz and begin to shine bright; at this point in time if you were not already at home or at least on your front porch you were in trouble. In other words, we all knew that when the streetlights come on it's time to be home, out of the darkness

and in the light and safety of home. Believers guess

what, the streetlights are on and it is time to come

out of the darkness and dwell in the marvelous light

of Jesus Christ.

1 Peter 2:1-3

Therefore, rid yourselves of all malice and all deceit,

hypocrisy, envy, and slander of every kind. Like newborn

babies, crave pure spiritual milk, so that by it you may grow

up in your salvation, now that you have tasted that the Lord

is good.

You have a right to be free from the onslaught of

the enemy and all his devices. What do we need to

do now?

2 Chronicles 7:14

If my people, which are called by my name, shall humble themselves, and pray, and seek my face, and turn from their wicked ways; then will I hear from heaven, and will forgive their sin, and will heal their land.

Pastors and church leaders take step back, look at what you are doing and why you are doing it and be certain that what goes on 'Behind the Cross' in your ministry is in line with God's plan. Shalom.

Jude 1:24-25

Now unto him that is able to keep you from falling, and to present you faultless before the presence of his glory with exceeding joy, to the only wise God our Savior, be glory and majesty, dominion and power, both now and ever. Amen.

About The Author

Minister Harvey L. Jones is an Ordained Minister of the Gospel of Jesus the Christ Minister Jones retired with the rank of Master Sergeant from the U. S. Marines after serving for over 20 years in various posts and stations throughout the globe. Minister Jones has been married to his Gadsden High school sweetheart, Linda K. Nelson for over 46 years. Linda and Harvey have four children and two grandchildren.

www.ingramcontent.com/pod-product-compliance
Lightning Source LLC
Chambersburg PA
CBHW031042110426
42740CB00046B/708